Once upon a time, there was a young boy. His name was Aladdin and he lived in China with his mother. They were very poor.

One day, a rich man came to Aladdin's house. He gave Aladdin a magic ring.

"Would you like to work for me?" he asked Aladdin.

"Oh yes," said Aladdin, "because we're very poor!"

The man took Aladdin to a cave. "Go down into the cave," he said, "and find my magic lamp!"

Aladdin was scared because the man was very angry now. "Oh, Oh!" said Aladdin very quietly, "he is a *bad* old man!"

Aladdin went down into the cave. It was
very dark and very cold. He looked for
the magic lamp, but he could not see it.
Then he turned a corner and jumped!
"Wooow!" said Aladdin.

There was a beautiful room, with a tree
and jewels, and ... the magic lamp.

3

Aladdin took the magic lamp.
"Give me my lamp!" said the bad old man
when he saw Aladdin. His eyes were big and
angry. But Aladdin was a very clever boy.
"Let me out first!" he said.
"Nooo!" said the man, and he shut Aladdin
in the cave.

Aladdin was scared, but then he remembered the ring.
"Hmm," he said, "this is a magic ring."
He looked at it, he smelled it, he tasted it, and ... nothing! But then he rubbed it and *Woosh!* a big green genie flew out.
"I'm the genie of the ring!" he said.

"What can I do for you?" he asked, "You can have anything you want!"

"I'd like to see my mother," said Aladdin.

*Woosh!* He was in his mother's kitchen. "This is a surprise!" said his mother, "but what's that dirty old thing you've got?" " ... let me clean it," she said.

*Woosh!* A big red genie flew out of the lamp!
"I'm the genie of the lamp!" he said, "What
can I do for you?"
"I'd like some money and a new house for
my mother," said Aladdin.

And *Woosh!* - they were rich!

Now Aladdin was a handsome young man.
One day he went to the city with his mother and he saw a beautiful young woman.
"She's nice!" said Aladdin, "I'm going to marry her!"
"She's the Emperor's daughter," said his mother,
"You can't marry her!"
"Watch this!" said Aladdin ...

... He rubbed the lamp and *Woosh!* they were in the Emperor's castle with the Emperor and his daughter.

"Hmm," said the Emperor, "you're a very handsome man. Are you rich?" he asked.

"Oh, yes," said Aladdin, "I'm very rich!"

"Then you can marry my daughter!" smiled the Emperor.

Aladdin lived in a big castle with his wife.

One morning, when Aladdin was not
there, a man came to the castle.
"New lamps for old!" he said.
"We've got an old lamp!" said Aladdin's
wife, ...I'd like a new one please."
And she gave the man the magic lamp.

But it was the bad old man!
"Aha!" he said happily, "now I have my magic lamp!"
He quickly rubbed it and *Woosh!* The big red genie flew out. The man pointed to Aladdin's castle and he said, "Take that castle and put it in the middle of the forest!"

Aladdin was very angry when he could
not find his castle.
"That bad old man ..." he said and he
rubbed his magic ring.
*Whoosh!* The big green genie flew out
of the ring.
"What can I do for you?" he said.
"Find my castle!" said Aladdin, "and
bring it here!"

And - *Whoosh!* - there was Aladdin's castle again.
Aladdin ran into the castle and saw the bad old
man. Aladdin was very fast and he quickly
caught the old man. He took the magic lamp
and rubbed it.
"I don't want to see this man again," he said.

"Now we can be happy!" Aladdin said, "but let's be careful with this lamp!"

When they looked at the lamp, they remembered the bad old man. But they did not see him again. Aladdin, his wife, and his mother lived happily ever after.

# ACTIVITIES

**Before you read**

Look at this picture about Aladdin and the Lamp, then try to answer the questions.

1. Can you:
(a) point to Aladdin?
(b) point to Aladdin's mother?
(c) point to a rich man?
(d) point to jewels?

2. Can you see:
(a) gold?
(b) a bag?
(c) a smile?
(d) a bad old man?

**After you read**

Match a line in "A" with a line in "B". One has been done for you.

| A | B |
|---|---|
| (1) Aladdin was a | out of the lamp. |
| The genie flew | a new house. |
| The bad old man was | very clever boy. |
| I'd like | marry her. |
| I'm going to | it was very dark. |
| Aladdin was scared because | very angry. |

**Pearson Education Limited**
Edinburgh Gate, Harlow,
Essex CM20 2JE, England
and Associated Companies throughout the world.

ISBN 978-0-582-43254-3

First published by Librairie du Liban Publishers, 1996
This adaptation first published 2000 under licence by Penguin Books
© 2000 Penguin Books
Illustrations © 1996 Librairie du Liban

12

Aladdin and the Lamp, Level 2
Retold by Marie Crook
Series Editors: Annie Hughes and Melanie Williams
Design by Neil Alexander, Monster Design
Illustrations by Angus McBride

*All rights reserved; no part of this publication may be reproduced, stored in a retrieval system, or transmitted in any form or by any means, electronic, mechanical, photocopying, recording or otherwise, without the prior writte permission of the Publishers.*

Printed in China
SWTC/12

Published by Pearson Education Limited in association with Penguin Books Ltd,
both companies being subsidiaries of Pearson Plc

For a complete list of the titles available in the Penguin Young Readers series please write to your local Pearson Education office or to: Penguin Readers Marketing Department, Pearson Education, Edinburgh Gate, Harlow, Essex CM20 2JE